BRITAIN
IN OLD PHOTOGRAPHS

MADE IN DARLINGTON

CHARLIE EMETT

Sutton Publishing Limited
Phoenix Mill · Thrupp · Stroud
Gloucestershire · GL5 2BU

First published 2003

Copyright © Charlie Emett, 2003

Title page photograph: The offices of the *Northern Echo*.
Front endpaper: Workers at the North Road Shops just before the start of the First World War.
Back endpaper: Wool being spun at Patons and Baldwins, 1966.

British Library Cataloguing in Publication Data
A catalogue record for this book is available from the British Library.

ISBN 0-7509-3086-1

Typeset in 10.5/13.5 pt Photina.
Typesetting and origination by
Sutton Publishing Limited.
Printed and bound in England by
J.H. Haynes & Co. Ltd, Sparkford.

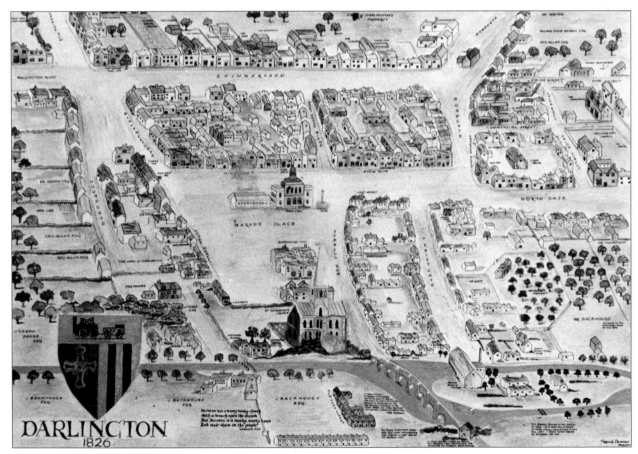

When the Stockton & Darlington Railway opened on 27 September 1825, it set the pattern for industrial development in Darlington which, as this map dated 1826 shows, was primarily a market town at that time.

CONTENTS

ACKNOWLEDGEMENTS

For allowing me to peruse the *Northern Echo*'s picture library, a most enjoyable occupation, my very special thanks go to David Kelly, managing director of the *Northern Echo*, and to Peter Barron, editor of this great daily of the north. Thank you, Christine Watson, lovely guardian of these archives. As ever, you are a dab hand at anticipating the need for a stimulating beverage. All images are courtesy of the *Northern Echo* apart from those in Chapter 3, which are from the Cleveland Bridge Company. To Gay Beer and Malcolm Scott of Cleveland Bridge, my sincere thanks for your kindness and valued help. You have much of which to be proud at Cleveland Bridge. Thank you Pam Gibson of Eagle Graphic for transforming my scrawl into floppy disc materials. It is always a real pleasure working with Sutton Publishing's brilliant editorial team, all good friends, all harmoniously pulling in the same direction: senior editors Simon Fletcher and Sarah Moore, editors Michelle Tilling, Anne Bennett and Alison Flowers, publishing co-ordinator Joyce Percival and PR specialist Rebecca Nicholls. It is a real privilege to be part of such a strong and very professional team. If I have omitted to thank anyone, it is inadvertent and I apologise. I must be responsible for something, and I am. Any errors are mine.

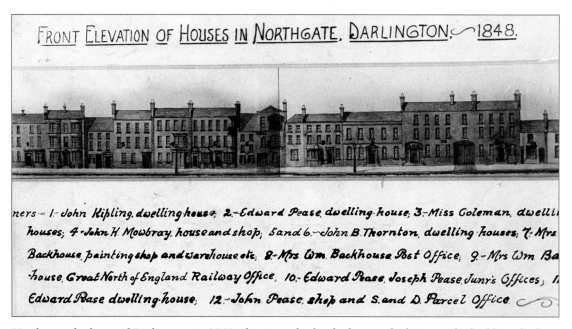

Northgate, the heart of Darlington, in 1848, showing who lived where and what uses the buildings had.

INTRODUCTION

The Saxon settlement of Darlington, spelt variously throughout the centuries as Dearlington, Dearnington, Dearington, Dernington, Darington and Darlington, may mean the 'tun' (village or homestead) of Dornod's people, the secluded 'tun' or the 'tun' on the watermeadows. Another theory is that the River Skerne, which Darlington straddles, was once called the Darnington, thus giving Darlington another alternative name, Darnington. Darlington was not mentioned in the Domesday Book because William I's commissioners, sent out in 1086 to record and value the settlements in the Conqueror's new realm, did not venture north of the River Tees.

During the Middle Ages English merchants exported their wool to Flanders, which had a valuable cloth industry. The wool was channelled through specific ports known as 'staples', where customs duty was paid. One wool merchant was John Durham of Darlington, who was paid 5 marks per wool sack. This was the lowest rate for wool, the highest being 10 marks a sack for Lincolnshire wool. John Durham received his purchase orders through the Bishop of Durham. They totalled 500 sacks of wool, and this deal established Darlington as an important wool centre.

A charter, long since lost, is thought to have been granted to Darlington by the Bishop of Durham towards the end of the twelfth century. (It was certainly in existence by the early thirteenth century.) The charter brought many benefits both to the bishop and to the town. The market not only provided a steady income for the bishop as the holder of the rights, but also stimulated trade and brought prosperity to the freeholders of the town, who were exempt from paying market tolls. It was the responsibility of the bailiff and his deputy to collect the tolls, which had to be paid on all goods bought and sold. Rules governing the conduct of the market and the quality of the goods sold there were laid down by the borough court.

By the sixteenth century butchers were selling meat from an area at the top of Darlington Market Place called 'the Shambles'. They also had a row of permanent stalls there, where the imprudent disposal of offal was a constant source of trouble. Fishmongers traded alongside the butchers in equally unhygienic conditions. Also trading from open stalls were people selling other foodstuffs, including bread, oatmeal, ginger bread, nuts, lemons, oranges and other fruits. Other merchants sold linen and woollen clothes, stockings, linen and milliners' goods. At Skinhill, near the Shambles, the skinners had their special area and the leather trade was well represented in the town by the fellmongers who dealt in animal skins and hides.

Monday was, and remains, market day, and livestock was sold at special fair days (or 'Great Mondays'), held throughout the year. Cattle sold at these special marts were exempt from tolls. The Mondays before and after May Day and Martinmas became hiring days for servants. As the wages offered by prospective employers were virtually the same, the big question for those being hired was 'Is it a good grub shop?'

As early as 1138 Darlington had a woollen industry. By 1383 there was a fulling mill on the River Skerne and a dyehouse was in existence. Cloth was sold in Darlington market and the town's merchants were doing a brisk trade exporting wool to Flanders. However, by the beginning of the sixteenth century cloth production in Darlington was in decline. The Bishop of Durham now received no rent from his dyehouse in Darlington because 'no dyers exist there'. Weaving was still carried out by the town's weavers, who had both linen and woollen looms. In October 1745 the Duke of Cumberland's army, 10,000 strong, passed through Darlington, and the town's Quaker woollen manufacturers presented every soldier with a flannel waist-coat free of charge.

Thomas Cauldwell was a Darlington woolcomber during the sixteenth century. His nephew Edward Pease (1711–85) worked for him, and when Thomas retired Edward took over the running of the business, expanding it to encompass dyeing and weaving. When Edward Pease died, his son Joseph became responsible for the Pease Mills on the River Skerne. The Pease family's interest in the textile industry continued to expand, their two Skerne-side mills being supplemented by the building of their Railway Mill, north of the town, close to the line of the Stockton & Darlington Railway. By 1851 Henry Pease & Co., with one cotton and two woollen mills, was one of Darlington's major employers. At the Great Exhibition of that year, Pease's Coburg cloth won a prestigious prize despite strong competition, and the company also provided the flags that decorated the exterior of the Crystal Palace.

For a great many years Darlington's prosperity had depended on its status as a market town, and on the production of leather and woollen and linen cloth. The wealth of the town's two principal families had been founded on wool and flax respectively, but where the Pease family's interest in the textile industry expanded, the Backhouse family soon diversified into banking. The first reference to banking in Darlington was an advertisement in the *Darlington Pamphlet* in 1772. Darlington banker J. Clement announced that he would exchange Portuguese gold for guineas or London drafts, the equivalent of banknotes. There was a shortage of English gold coins at this time and many Portuguese gold coins had been accepted in payment of debts.

James Backhouse and his eldest son Jonathan established a private bank, James & Jonathan Backhouse, in Northgate in 1774. Jonathan was later to become the first treasurer of the Stockton & Darlington Railway. In 1778 the bank ran into problems when forgeries of its banknotes appeared in the town. The culprit was caught and executed the following year. When James Backhouse died in 1798, the name of the bank was changed to Jonathan Backhouse & Company.

The most famous episode in the bank's history concerned the Earl of Darlington of Raby Castle. In an attempt to make the bank insolvent, he instructed all his tenants to pay their rents in Backhouse notes. When Jonathan Backhouse heard of this, he rushed to London to obtain sufficient bullion to cover the value of the notes when they were presented by the earl. On the return journey, the coach lost a wheel at Croft. Anxious not to waste precious time on repairs, Jonathan Backhouse redistributed the gold to counter-balance the coach and completed the journey on three wheels! When the banknotes were presented for payment by the earl's agent, he was told to inform his master that if he should ever wish to sell Raby, payment would be made in the same metal.

When the Stockton & Darlington Railway was opened on 27 September 1825, it marked the beginning of the Industrial Revolution, which brought with it developments that would change Darlington out of all recognition.

1

North Road Shops

THE FIRST LOCOMOTIVE TO BE BUILT IN NORTH ROAD SHOPS DARLINGTON
CONTRACTOR BUILT 1864

The opening of the Stockton & Darlington Railway on 27 September 1825 set the pattern for the development of a railway system throughout the world, and part of this growth was the creation at Darlington of the LNER workshops at North Road, Stooperdale and Faverdale. Locomotives were built at North Road and Stooperdale while Faverdale produced railway wagons. Built in 1864, no. 175 Contractor, an 0–6–0, was the first locomotive to be built in North Road Shops. It marked the beginning of an industry that grew steadily until by 1930 54 locomotives and 4,200 wagons were being built at Darlington annually.

The number of men initially employed at North Road Shops is not known but after eighteen months there were 273 and by 1866 339. By the 1890s there were 1,400, and the numbers remained fairly constant thereafter. This photograph of workmen at North Road Shops was taken just before the outbreak of the First World War. The boys in the picture are all aged about 14 years and are in their first jobs.

Between the 1890s and the outbreak of the First World War in 1914 more buildings appeared in North Road, including a brass foundry, coppersmiths' shop, stores and a machine shop. In 1903 the erecting shop pictured here was built. It was 500 ft long and 200 ft wide and contained seventy-two pits in three bays, which remained in use until the works closed and were demolished in 1981.

During the First World War locomotive building slowed down as North Road Shops concentrated on producing shells. In August 1915 the government-financed Darlington National Projectile Factory was opened. NER managed the operation on the understanding that after the war it would take over the factory along with any of the fixed plant and machinery that would be useful for railway engineering. More than a thousand women staffed the factory, which produced more than 1½ million shells and repaired more than a million cartridge cases. After the war the building of locomotives was stepped up. In 1929 the magnificent Hush Hush engine, displayed here by Reginald Moses who worked on it, was built at North Road Shops.

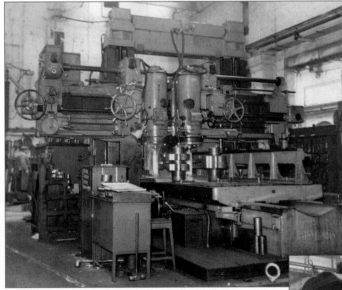

This Kendall Gent profiling and channelling drilling machine can drill four locomotive coupling rods at the same time.

Pictured here in 1954, this is one of the 2,775 locomotives built at North Road Shops between 1863 and 1981.

The old and the new. *Above*: Locomotive no. 84029, pictured in immaculate condition in October 1957, along with some of the people involved in its construction, was the last steam locomotive to be built at North Road Shops. *Below*: In contrast, this is diesel engine no. D5094, the first of eighty-five main-line diesel-electric locomotives built in Darlington, which was completed in February 1960.

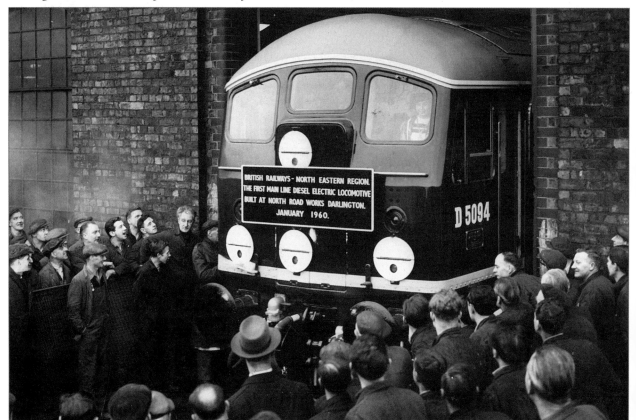

Locomotive no. 65662 meeting its end at North Road Shops. It was scrapped in June 1960.

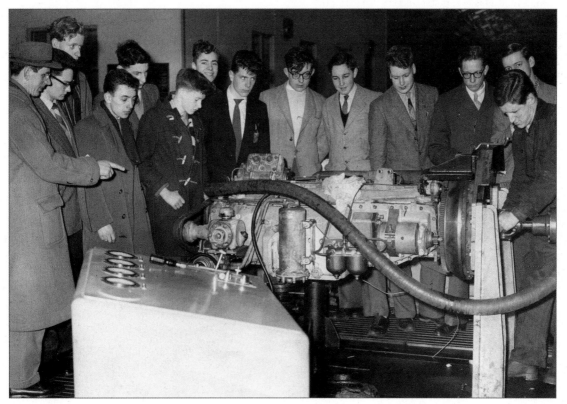

With the advent of diesel locomotives came new construction techniques. Here, in 1960, equipment in the diesel engine testing shop at North Road works is being explained to apprentices.

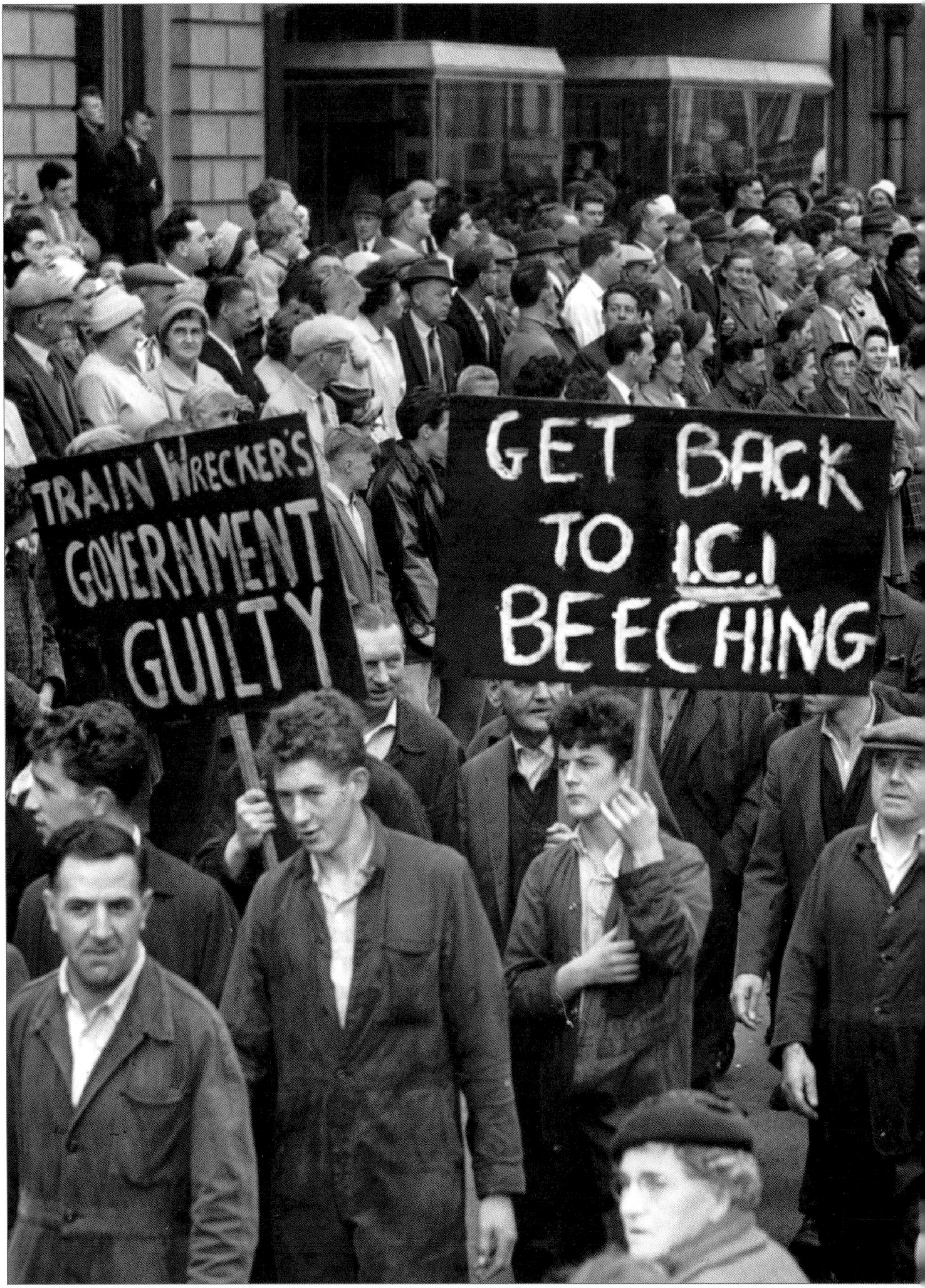
TRAIN WRECKER'S
GOVERNMENT
GUILTY
GET BACK
TO I.C.I
BEECHING

On the signs:

DOWN WITH THE TORIES AND BEECHING

BEECHING'S TACTICS

SACK BEECHING ... THE REASON WHY WE ARE OUT IN FORCE IS BECAUSE THE TORIES ARE TAKING THE WRONG COURSE

In 1948 Darlington began building its finest engines, the 'Peppercorn Pacifics', the first of which was no. 60130, later named *Kestrel*. Those involved were filled with justifiable pride and the atmosphere was euphoric at North Road Shops where they were built. By 1960 the mood had changed as Beeching's axe hung over North Road Shops. On 28 July 1962 a deputation from Darlington went to see Dr Beeching to plead, unsuccessfully, for the future of North Road Shops.

A protest march against the closure of North Road Shops was held on 4 September 1962. The Mayor of Darlington is one of the speakers addressing the marchers. *Inset*: The deputation from Darlington who went to see Dr Beeching to plead for the survival of North Road Shops.

The workforce leaving North Road Shops on 20 September 1962, hoping that it is not for the last time.

Times may be hard in 1962, but all doom and gloom spells misery. So, despite an uncertain future for North Road Shops, the carnival participants set out to bring laughter into a lacklustre year. In so doing, they pour happiness over themselves.

Between 1958 and 1959 locomotive production at North Road Shops was restricted to shunter engines. However, between February 1960 and September 1964, eighty-five main-line diesel-electric locomotives were scheduled to be built at North Road Shops. Over these years cleaner facilities were introduced for the diesels. Yet, despite this, the end of locomotion production at North Road Shops was beginning to look inevitable. Moreover, the withdrawal of steam locomotives meant that repair work was declining. So when a one-day strike was called on 3 October 1962, those involved knew that the long-term prospects of employment at North Road Shops were poor. Their livelihood was on the line.

In a desperate bid to remain viable, North Road Shops cut up many LMS engines and other types of engine that had never previously been seen at the site, in addition to demolishing NER engines. But the threat of closure still loomed large. On 9 March 1964 the workforce staged a protest march. One sentence on one banner highlights their heartfelt plea: 'All we ask is one year.'

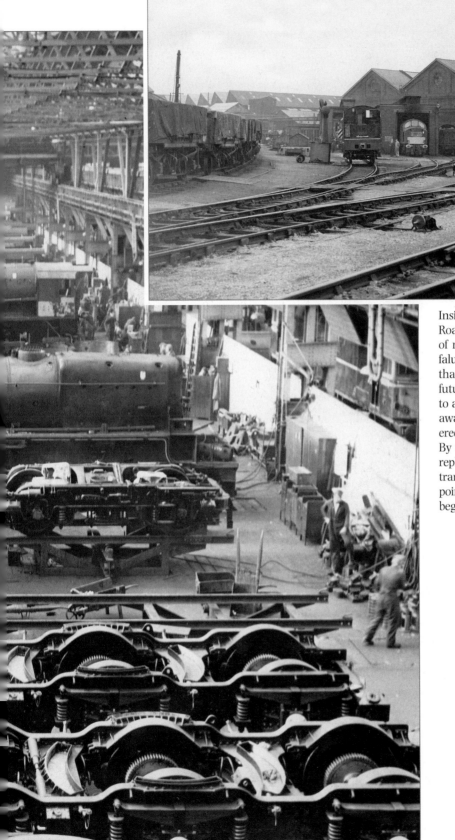

Inside the erecting shops at North Road Shops, 1964. It was not the stuff of romance and it was not some high-falutin' fancy. It was much more basic than that: it was work, hope for the future and security. It was not much to ask for, but it was already slipping away. *Inset*: The entrance to the main erecting shops, 24 September 1962. By this time diesel power was already replacing steam. It was a smooth transition, and there was no specific point where one stopped and the other began.

Darlington's North Road Shops delegation anxiously awaiting the outcome of a meeting at British Railways' headquarters in Marylebone, London, on 10 March 1964. Left to right: Tom Hoy (NUR no. 2), Jim Leathead (boilersmith and Confederation representative), John McGuire (AEU), Fred Jaques (AEU), Sidney Wheeler (AEU), Dick Thornley (AEU) and Norman Temple (AEU). Mr Temple was the delegation's spokesman on the day.

Meanwhile, back in Darlington, the North Road Shops workforce waited for news. The prospects were not good.

Inside North Road Shops, the repair of locomotives continued as the remaining workforce pinned their hopes on a last-minute upturn of fortunes that would save their jobs.

NOTICE

IN CONSULTATION WITH THE TRADE UNIONS IT HAS BEEN DECIDED THAT THE FUTURE PLANNING SHOULD BE MADE KNOWN IN THOSE WORKS WHICH WILL CONTINUE AND THOSE WORKS WHICH ARE SCHEDULED FOR CLOSURE. SO FAR AS DARLINGTON NORTH ROAD AND STOOPERDALE ARE CONCERNED, A DECISION HAS BEEN TAKEN THAT THESE WORKS WILL CONTINUE UNTIL 1965 AND THEREAFTER BE CLOSED.

SPECIAL MEASURES WILL BE TAKEN TO REDUCE HARDSHIP CREATED BY REDUNDANCY AND THE UNDER-NOTED ARE THE TERMS WHICH HAVE BEEN IMPROVED AS A RESULT OF REPRESENTATION BY THE TRADE UNIONS, AND THESE ARE BEING FURTHER CONSIDERED BY THEM.

NOT LESS THAN SIX MONTHS NOTICE WILL BE GIVEN BEFORE THE FIRST DISCHARGES NECESSARY FOR CLOSURE START TO OPERATE. TO HELP OLDER MEN, AND MEN IN DIFFICULT EMPLOYMENT AREAS, LONGER NOTICE THAN SIX WEEKS TO BE GIVEN WHENEVER POSSIBLE. TO SUCH CASES RESETTLEMENT LUMP SUM PAYMENTS TO BE PAID TO MEN WISHING TO LEAVE UP TO THE FOLLOWING MAXIMUM PERIODS PRIOR TO NORMAL DISCHARGE DATES:—

PERIOD

AGE ON LEAVING RAILWAY SERVICE. I.	GENERAL RULE AT ALL WORKS OTHER THAN THOSE IN COL. III 2	MEN EMPLOYED AT GLASGOW, DARLINGTON, WALKER GATE EARLESTOWN & HORWICH WORKS. III
UP TO 40 YEARS	6 WEEKS	10 WEEKS
40 TO 50	8 WEEKS	12 WEEKS
50 TO UNDER 55	10 WEEKS	14 WEEKS
55 AND OVER	12 WEEKS	AT ANY TIME AFTER NOTICE OF CLOSURE OF THEIR WORKS HAS BEEN ANNOUNCED.

IN ADDITION TO THESE MEASURES SPECIAL FACILITIES IN VARIOUS WAYS ARE BEING GIVEN TO HELP MEN TO OBTAIN OTHER EMPLOYMENT, AND DETAILS CAN BE GIVEN ON REQUEST.

The long-expected but dreaded news was announced on 20 September 1965, when this redundancy notice was displayed at North Road and Stooperdale Shops.

Despite the redundancy notices, obligations still had to be met and some work remained to keep the workforce busy. They still took pride in a job well done, as this picture dated 1 October 1965 shows, but the enthusiasm was on the wane.

Pictured here on 2 April 1966 are some of the twenty-three workmen from the stores department who dismantled and removed the last of the machinery at Darlington's North Road Shops. On 1 April 1966 the works closed officially, and when the twenty-three workmen from the stores department collected their pay they found that they had all been paid at a lower rate – as much as £200 less – than that stipulated on their redundancy payment forms. The cats were not too happy either – they got no redundancy milk! What an ignominious end to North Road Shops.

North Road Shops in January 1969, forlorn and deserted. It was offered for sale by local estate agents Sanderson, Townend and Gilbert on behalf of British Rail at £350,000, exclusive of travelling cranes, machinery and railway track. In the late 1970s the site was purchased by William Morrison Supermarkets Ltd.

Someone asked if the clock that hung outside the North Road Shops, pictured here on 25 November 1966, could be placed elsewhere in Darlington to commemorate the hundred years of Darlington's contribution to railway history. The request was refused, a British Railways' spokesman at York informing all and sundry that the clock, along with all the property, was up for sale. Because the clock was part of the sale, its future was in the hands of the purchaser.

2

Whessoe

In 1790 the Quaker William Kitching opened an ironmonger's shop in Tubwell Row, right in the middle of Darlington. From these small beginnings grew Whessoe, the international group of companies that became world leaders in the field of engineering. For over 200 years the group has designed and manufactured every type of engineering product from small castings for the Stockton & Darlington Railway to huge components for nuclear power stations. Seen here in 1894 is the first oil storage tank built by Whessoe for the Anglo-American Oil Company (later Esso). This tank had a capacity of 1,000,000 gallons.

By 1830 it was clear that the Tubwell Row foundry site was too small and the business was transferred to a new site a mile to the north. At that time the railway was the foundry's main customer, although orders were also received from various collieries, the local gas works and neighbourhood mills. In about 1910 the Whessoe foundry, as it was now called, supplied 50,000 tons of cast and wrought ironwork for the Edgware Road–Baker Street extension of the London Underground, seen here.

As early as 1902 Whessoe was producing storage tanks up to 110 ft in diameter, and the total capacity of the tanks produced annually by Whessoe was about 50,000,000 gallons. Thomas Coates and his son Alfred, who succeeded him as managing director in 1911, lifted Whessoe into the front ranks of engineering firms in the north-east. They were generous to their workmen and treated them well. In return, the staff were expected to work as hard as they did. By 1920 the Coates family had built up connections with the oil, gas and chemical industries. Pictured here, in October 1962, are some of the Whessoe-built storage tanks at the Esso refinery at Fawley in Hampshire, used to contain intermediate and finished lubricating oils. Each tank has a total capacity of 28,000 tons.

The frame for a 140-ft-diameter dome roof tank under construction at the Hellenic Petroleum Refinery at Aspropyrgos in April 1963. Whessoe acted in a design and supervisory capacity for Hellenic Shipyards, whose contract from the Hellenic Petroleum Refinery was valued at approximately £¼ million.

This reactor pressure vessel, pictured on 29 January 1963, was designed and constructed by Whessoe for Latina Nuclear Power Station, situated some 40 miles from Rome. It was built by the Nuclear Power Group in close cooperation with AGIP Nucleare, Italy.

This three-compartment, glass-reinforced resin tanker was built by Whessoe for pressure discharge, and contained 4,100 gallons. Pictured here on 13 November 1963, the tanker was exhibited at the Scottish Motor Show in Glasgow that year.

This pressure vessel, pictured on 9 December 1963, was the last to be dispatched in a series of orders that Whessoe received from the South-Western Gas Board. The vessel is 9 ft in diameter with an overall length of 65 ft and can be used to store butane at a temperature not exceeding 113°F. Built of ½-in thick steel, each 'bullet' has been designed to withstand a pressure of 100 lb/sq. in.

This Whessoe-built air mixing sphere, pictured on 9 December 1963, is part of a complex system of pipework for conveying air via a compressing and heating plant to a 'cell' in which large jet aircraft engines are tested under varying simulated flight conditions at the National Gas Turbine Establishment, Pyestock.

This double-shell sphere, pictured on 30 January 1964, was designed and built by Whessoe at the Fawley Refinery for the storage of liquid ethylene at a working temperature of minus 155°F. It is thought to be the largest liquid ethylene storage sphere ever built.

When a pressure vessel leaves Whessoe it tends to hog the road! This massive tank, pictured on 4 August 1964, was on the first stage of its journey to Saudi Arabia via Teesmouth.

The floating roof storage tanks behind the completed 43-ft 6-in-diameter spheres were designed, fabricated and erected by Whessoe at the Regent Refining Co. Ltd's refinery near Pembroke in South Wales. When it was opened by Queen Elizabeth the Queen Mother on 15 October 1964 it was the largest oil storage installation in the United Kingdom and Whessoe had a £1½ million share in it. Whessoe supplied and erected thirty-four floating roof tanks, including six circular tanks of 190 ft in diameter and four 43-ft 6-in-diameter spheres. To do the job as quickly as possible, forty specially adapted trains carried about 16,000 tons of fabricated steelwork from Whessoe's Darlington works.

A Whessoe-built treater for one of the crude-oil conditioning plants at Upper Assam in India, being unloaded at Calcutta Docks in 1965. It was to form part of the East's second-largest crude-oil pipeline.

Prominent features of the first stage of the Eastern Gas Board's Hitchin Gas Reforming Works, opened on 2 June 1965 by the Minister of Power, Rt Hon. Frederick James Erroll MP, were these three 40-ft 6-in-diameter Whessoe storage spheres, supported on columns.

Moving a giant reactor vessel, 31 ft long and 18 ft wide, can be a complicated business! When this one left Whessoe's Darlington plant on 26 November 1968, telegraph poles, bollards and street lamps all had to be moved out of the way. It was not the longest load to leave Whessoe but it was probably the widest – and the problems were caused by its width. It was the first of three vessels built for the new ICI plant at Wilton.

A 600-ton Whessoe-built steel reactor liner being moved into its final position at Hunterston 'B' Nuclear Power Station in 1972. The liner is 63 ft high and 62 ft in diameter. Hunterston 'B' Nuclear Power Station was being built by the Nuclear Power Group Ltd for the South of Scotland Electricity Board.

Clive Denn, a student engineer at Whessoe, explaining one of his company's products to a party of Czechoslovakian engineering students when they visited the Whessoe works at Darlington in July 1969, during their stay on Teesside.

Overleaf: An aerial view of Whessoe's Darlington works, 1970.

Some of the executives of Whessoe Ltd, 3 July 1970. Between them they share heavy responsibilities. Left to right: Mr D.S. Hudspeth (marketing director), Mr J.H. Davies (financial director), Mr W. Smart (Group chief executive), Lord Erroll (chairman), Mr R. Slater (production director), Mr D.J.T. Outrim (managing director, Aiton and Co. Ltd) and Mr A. Nelson (director and general manager, construction).

Sir Joseph Nwankwu (centre), a newly appointed director of Whessoe Engineering of Nigeria, is seen here on 2 October 1974 with Mr William Smart, Whessoe Group chief executive (right) and Mr G. Ranwick, Whessoe Group secretary. It was Sir Joseph's first visit to Darlington.

Part of the Whessoe display at
the International Shipping
Exhibition in Oslo, 14–30 May
1965. Whessoe is certainly not
backwards in coming forwards
and it has much of which to be
proud.

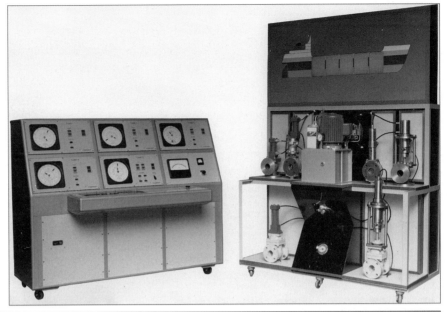

Mr Ken Prest (left), contracts manager for Whessoe Ltd, discussing with Mr Philip Prydz of Skarpenord, Oslo, the finer
points of a new valve for liquefied natural gas at Whessoe's stand at the International Shipping Exhibition in Oslo in
May 1965.

The heaviest load ever to be moved on rubber wheels, a module built
for British Petroleum by Whessoe of Darlington, is seen here leaving
Teesside on 23 July 1975. The 260-ft-long unit, weighing 1,200 tons,
was moved on 4 100-wheeled bogies.

For the third time in seven years Whessoe, with its workforce of 1,400, won the Golden Hand Safety award in 1981. Here, Brian Rowland, Whessoe's general manager, is pictured (left) receiving the award from W.B. Lester, the safety adviser of the North of England Engineering Employers Association, watched by some of the Whessoe workforce.

Mr Ron Bishop, pictured here on 30 December 1986, on his retirement as managing director of Whessoe Ltd.

Whessoe computing systems wizards, pictured on 14 April 1990 in happy mood. Left to right: Mike Hobdel, Stuart Dean, Keith Berry and John Richardson. They are jubilant because they have just discovered how to get Channel 4! Unfortunately, in 2002 Whessoe no longer has a presence in Darlington.

3

Cleveland Bridge

In 1877 Henry Isaac Dixon bought an interest in a 2-acre site at Smithfield Road, Darlington, and in 1882 Charles Frederick Dixon bought it outright. He formed the Cleveland Bridge and Engineering Co. Ltd on 27 July 1898. This is the entrance to Cleveland's Smithfield Road site.

In 1893 the rapidly expanding Cleveland Bridge company built its first overseas bridge in New South Wales, Australia. This picture was taken during its construction. In the same year it also built a bridge over the River Negro/Amazon at Manaus in Brazil. In 1902 Cleveland Bridge won its first major contract, worth £600,000, for building the King Edward VII bridge over the River Tyne. This was followed in 1904 by its first significant overseas contract, worth £72,000, for the Victoria Falls bridge across the River Zambesi and the Blue Nile bridge at Khartoum in 1907.

Cleveland Bridge's Smithfield Road site looked much the same in 1980, when this picture was taken, as it did during the first sixty-odd years of its life. During that time almost all the work that left the Smithfield Road site was designed for riveting, not welding.

In the years before the Second World War many bridges were built by Cleveland Bridge in Africa, China, India, New Zealand and South America. The company also supplied 15,000 tons of bridge for the French railways. This map shows where Cleveland bridges were sited in India, and the date they were built.

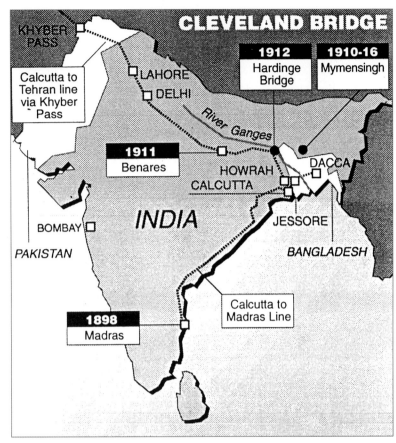

CLEVELAND BRIDGE

KHYBER PASS

Calcutta to Tehran line via Khyber Pass

LAHORE

DELHI

River Ganges

1912 Hardinge Bridge

1910-16 Mymensingh

1911 Benares

HOWRAH

CALCUTTA

DACCA

INDIA

JESSORE

BOMBAY

PAKISTAN

BANGLADESH

Calcutta to Madras Line

1898 Madras

Harding Bridge across the River Ganges in Bangladesh was built by Cleveland Bridge in 1912. It is an amazing 5,694 ft long!

Cleveland Bridge erected 250 tons of steelwork to support the huge glass roof of Coutts Bank, London, pictured here on 17 April 1977.

The Thames Barrier, pictured here in about 1978, was built to protect London from tidal surges from the North Sea. The steel gates and operating mechanisms were made by a consortium of the Cleveland Bridge and Engineering Company (Trafalgar House Group) and Davy-Loewy of Sheffield. Cleveland also installed the gates.

Sharon Lowther, pictured in November 1978, was Cleveland's first trainee draughtswoman.

The Bosporus bridge links the two halves of Turkey and also joins Europe to Asia. It was constructed in record time for the type of structure and its size, with a main span of 1,074 m. The thinness of the deck sections and the slenderness of the towers were important aesthetic features. In 1973, when it was opened to public traffic, it was the longest suspension bridge in Europe.

In 1967 C.C. Dixon, who had succeeded his father J.R. Dixon, decided that the future of the company would be best assured by becoming a subsidiary of a larger company and he arranged for the shares to be purchased by the Cementation Construction Group, later acquired by Trafalgar House. In 1972 Trafalgar House expanded its activities into the new offshore oil market and began to construct process modules. This business subsequently became Trafalgar Offshore Ltd. In January 1982 Cleveland moved from Smithfield Road to its present site. The transfer cost a staggering £26 million, supported by grants from the government and the EEC.

The present Cleveland Bridge site, pictured in 1982 when it opened.

In 1982 the Queen Elizabeth II bridge was built by Cleveland at Dartford.

The construction of the Humber bridge took eight years, during which time many thousands of tonnes of steel and concrete were used and upwards of a thousand workers and staff were employed at times of peak activity. The bridge was designed to cross the last major estuary in Britain. It comprises reinforced concrete towers, aerial-spun catenary cables and a continuously welded, closed-box road deck, supported by inclined hanger cables. The bridge is a masterpiece of civil engineering and its construction is very complex. When it was completed in 1981, it held the record for the longest span in the world, a record that remained unbroken until 1988. The first traffic crossed the bridge on 24 June 1981. The Humber bridge opened up, both socially and economically, two previously remote and insular areas of England.

Cleveland is renowned as a world leader in bridge building, but it is also heavily involved in other important projects. Canary Wharf, pictured here, was another Cleveland triumph.

Cleveland Bridge apprentices, pictured in 1988 with their reconstruction of Fowler's steam-powered plough.

Cleveland Bridge and Engineering Middle East is now the biggest supplier of cranes in the Middle East. Its main markets are container-handling cranes for port authorities and electric overhead travelling cranes for industrial customers.

New technology puts Cleveland at the forefront of bridge construction. Developing this state-of-the-art deck-welding machine has enabled the company to automate the assembly of orthotropic deck panels and increase production rates by more than four times. In 1993, when this picture was taken, it was the only one of its kind in existence and its £500,000 price tag demonstrates the company's commitment to maintaining its worldwide competitive edge in bridge construction.

Cleveland's steel helps to convert to a combined cycle operation a Middle East gas turbine at the Dubai Aluminium Company's smelter in 1993.

Mr Alan Gibson, Cleveland's production manager (right), and Mr James Blake, pictured at Cleveland's Darlington works on 14 January 1993, discuss a production problem during the early stages of the construction of the Tsing Ma bridge. Work commenced on the bridge in mid-1992 as part of Hong Kong's Airport core programme that comprised ten major projects to replace the territory's old airport at Kai Tak with a new one on Lantau Island.

Cleveland works on the principle that a streamlined production flow provides a better product and a faster delivery. The welder seen here in November 1996 is part of a tremendously efficient workforce.

In 1996 all the Trafalgar House companies, including the Cleveland Bridge and Engineering Co. Ltd, were acquired by Kvaerner. Cleveland became Kvaerner Cleveland Bridge and it was under that name that the Hong Kong Convention and Exhibition Centre, pictured here, was built in 1996.

The main span of the Tsing Ma bridge, seen here under construction in 1997, links Tsin Yi Island and Ma Wan Island. The distance between the two portal braced reinforced towers, each 206 m high, is 1,377 m. Key elements of the design are those relating to shipping and the typhoon season. High navigational clearance for Hong Kong harbour means the main span stands 79.45 m above mean high water. The structure is also able to withstand wind speeds of up to 300 km per hour. Completed in 1997, when this picture was taken, Tsing Ma bridge is one of the world's longest and most technically complex single-span structures with a total length between abutments of 2.17 km. It is also the world's longest suspension bridge, carrying both road and rail tracks on two decks.

4

Cummins

Since 1 February 1918, when the incorporation papers were filed for the Cummins Engine Company, Cummins has grown from a fledgling concern manufacturing what was then called 'a new kind of engine' to one of the USA's leading industrial corporations, whose engines are providing dependable power for over 700 different applications in nearly every country of the free world. In 1964 a Chrysler Cummins factory was erected at Darlington and in mid-1965 the Cummins Engine factory was built alongside it. Pictured here is a model of the Cummins Engine factory made before construction began.

The site on which the Cummins and Chrysler Cummins factories were to be built covered an area of 640,000 sq. ft, and it was hoped that they would provide almost 2,000 jobs for Darlington. In the background of the picture, on its 140,000 sq. ft site, is the Cummins Engines factory, intended to employ 700 men working on a patent pressure-time fuel system and diesel components. The factory was ready by the summer of 1965. The Chrysler Cummins factory, on its 500,000 sq. ft site, was designed to employ 1,250 men turning out diesel engines and was to be ready by November 1964. *Inset*: The Chrysler Cummins factory on 13 July 1965, proudly flying the Union Jack and the Stars and Stripes together as symbols of a great international partnership. On 23 April 1968 the Cummins Engines Company announced that it had agreed to buy out Chrysler from their joint operation of the Chrysler Cummins assembly plant at Darlington.

Cummins engines are sold and serviced in 125 countries throughout the world, and this number increases year by year. In about 1964 Cummins' Darlington factory began producing two new diesel power units, as seen here.

Chrysler International's sturdy 'Farmobil', built in 1964, combined the best features of rural utility and city delivery vehicles. It was developed at Darlington specially for use in countries requiring low cost transportation.

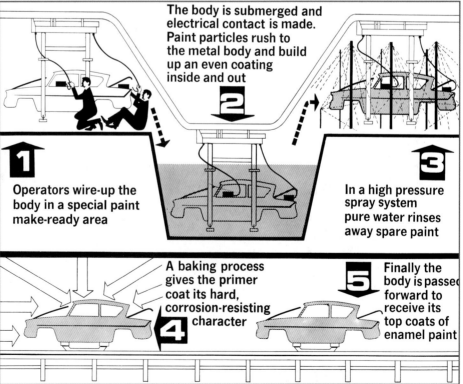

The body is submerged and electrical contact is made. Paint particles rush to the metal body and build up an even coating inside and out

2

1 Operators wire-up the body in a special paint make-ready area

3 In a high pressure spray system pure water rinses away spare paint

A baking process gives the primer coat its hard, corrosion-resisting character **4**

5 Finally the body is passed forward to receive its top coats of enamel paint

This illustrates the process used to cover a vehicle's body with a corrosion-resisting paint. This procedure is used in the Darlington factory.

Mr R. Foreman, secretary, points out interesting details to Councillor C. Spence, chairman of Darlington Development Committee (centre), and Councillor S. Oliver, during their informal visit to Chrysler Cummins Ltd on 25 March 1965.

A 200-ft jib crane lifts part of a chimney into place on the 90-ft-high silo at the Chrysler Cummins factory on 18 May 1965. The silo is used to extract fumes from the engine test-bed.

Inside the Cummins Engine factory, 14 July 1965. Inspectors patrolled the lines constantly, checking that vital components and engines being assembled were always protected from dust and dirt.

One of the Cummins-engined police patrol boats built by Brooke Marine for service in the West Indies, pictured here during speed trials in 1970.

On 25 June 1974 the Cummins Engine Company held its annual worldwide quality conference at the Europa Lodge Hotel, Darlington. From left to right: Mr Carl Stahl (Tennessee), Mr George Hollins (Columbus, Indiana), Mr Gordon Redshaw (Columbus, Indiana), Mr Alan Sunderland (Darlington), Mr Jim Carruthers (Darlington) and Mr Bob Bilz (Columbus, Indiana).

But all was not going so well at the Cummins factory site. Jobs were at risk and pickets were out, as seen in this picture, taken on 15 August 1974.

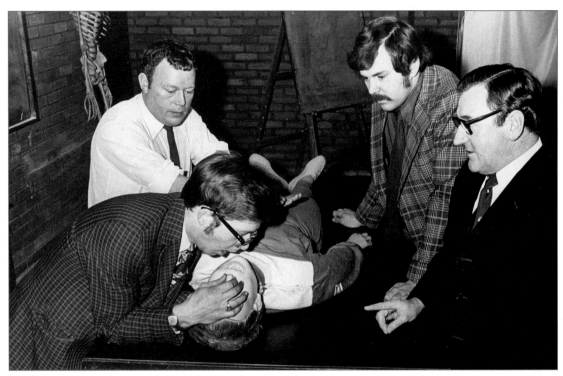

Pictured here on 9 December 1975, in the run-up to Christmas, these Cummins employees are either brushing up their first-aid techniques or learning an unusual variation of kissing under the mistletoe! (The character on the far left has overdone the pre-Christmas dieting.)

Smiles all round as Mr Stephen Cheetham, an assembly operator with Cummins Ltd, receives his prize, a picnic hamper, from Mr John Benson (left), area consultant with Protective Footwear Ltd, on 16 October 1975. Mr Cheetham was one of fifteen winners from over 10,000 entries in a national safety footwear competition. Watching are Mr Ken Davies (second left), manager of international personnel, and Mr Ken Harburn, Cummins' assistant safety officer.

Lord Barnard, the Lord Lieutenant of County Durham, and Mr J. Patrick of Cummins holding the Queen's Award for Exports, which was presented to the company on 3 November 1976.

Cummins' longest-serving machine operator, Nancy Walters, retired after thirteen years with the company. During her retirement party, where this picture was taken on 3 June 1980, she was presented with a scroll by her production line foreman, Allan Bruce. About ninety fellow workers watched the ceremony.

Under the sound leadership of managing director Mr Euan MacFarlane, pictured here in reflective mood in March 1982, Cummins Engineering Ltd became one of the country's leading exporters.

Later that same year, on 7 September 1982, Mr MacFarlane collected another Queen's Award for Export Achievement on behalf of Cummins Engineering Ltd. Also present, from left to right, were Councillor Bill Newton, Lord Barnard, the Lord Lieutenant of County Durham, and Mr Jim Gray, director of corporate personnel. Astonishingly, the following year Cummins won yet another Queen's Award for Export Achievement.

In February 1986 Cummins Engines revealed their new diesel engine, built for the new United Buses.

Cummins' basic product is power, and research into new forms of power has been and will continue to be the foundation of the company's growth. Like many other products power is subject to constant change and refinement under the spur of technological advances and competition. In fact, one chairman of Cummins Engines, Mr Irwin Miller, maintained that 'the only constant in business is change'. In this picture Mr Euan MacFarlane, as Vice-President of European Operations (1988–99), illustrates that point with one of the company's latest developments.

This bus, one of the most modern in United's fleet, is powered by a diesel engine specially produced for that purpose. Pictured here on 16 July 1986, Mr Terry Hogg, manager of the engine-making plant, was on hand to ensure that the Cummins-powered buses will run smoothly.

STOP
CUMMINS
FROM
GOING
IF YOU SEE SID TELL HIM
PLEASE
SIGN
CUMMINS
PETITION

In 1986 the Cummins workforce was faced with a situation no one could have predicted a couple of years earlier. Yet such are the uncertainties of commerce and trade that the unthinkable became reality. In December 1986 the company's workforce staged a protest march against the very real prospect of Cummins ceasing operations in Darlington.

Back in 1966 the Cummins Engines Company started an international training school at Darlington which became famous not only among Cummins diesel users but throughout the diesel industry. Staff instructors were capable of lecturing in all commercial languages, which meant that overall language coverage was better than that of any other European industrial training establishment. Training being of the essence, the company also nurtured apprentices, two of whom, Andrew Taylor and Paul Spooner, are pictured here on 25 April 1989, proudly displaying an engine they have renovated.

In July 1989 Cummins celebrated twenty-five years, 1964 to 1989, in Darlington. They presented the two anniversary cakes to Darlington's Glebe Road School, much to the delight of the children and staff there.

Two years on and Mr Denis Welch, plant manager of Cummins, Darlington, is pictured at the end of the production line of the 'B' series engine on 23 May 1991, to celebrate the manufacture of the 100,000th engine.

The interior of Cummins' factory, December 1991.

While this operator carefully adjusted his machine in about 1992, somebody was throwing a spanner in the works.

The interior of the closed component plant at Cummins' factory, June 1993. In 2002 Cummins still runs another factory in Darlington.

5

Cotton Wool

In 1946 the Carlisle firm of John Laing & Sons began work on a new factory for Messrs Patons and Baldwins Ltd on a 140-acre site at Lingfield Lane, Darlington. The contract price was well over £1 million for the building of administrative offices and a factory. The contract was later extended to include a housing estate adjoining the works. The factory was intended to concentrate on the manufacture of hand-knitting yarns that had previously been made in mills at Halifax, Wakefield, Leicester and Melton Mowbray, and about three-thousand people, one-third of them men, were to be employed there. A limited number of key workers would be brought in from other mills, the rest being recruited locally. In 1948 an engine was built that became Patons and Baldwins' very own, as this picture shows.

Addressing a meeting at Halifax on 14 October 1946, Mr Philip A. Wright, vice-chairman of Patons and Baldwins, described the new Darlington factory. 'In our planning,' he said, 'every effort has been made to lighten the work of the operatives and we have not the slightest intention of asking them to undertake more work than they can easily manage.' *Above*: the steam dye vat, pictured in October 1959, was part of Patons and Baldwins' new factory, which was the largest of its kind in the United Kingdom and almost certainly the largest in the world. It was mainly of single-storey construction for ease in organising the flow of material from one process to another. The factory covered an area of some 34 acres, the remaining 106 acres of the site being allocated to houses for key employees, an administrative block containing a training centre for operatives, lecture rooms, offices for the personnel manager, doctor, dentist, chiropodist, nursing staff, etc., a canteen to seat 2,000, a concert hall with stage and dressing rooms and a projection room for films, and 25 acres of playing grounds containing 2 full-size cricket pitches, 12 tennis courts and 2 bowling greens. *Left*: Some cheery employees relaxing in the factory garden, 31 August 1961.

Visitors from overseas inspecting samples of wool, 19 October 1961.

Patons had a busy apprenticeship scheme. It trained technical apprentices for four years and craft apprentices for five or six years. Pictured here on 18 April 1961 are four apprentices 'on the shop floor'.

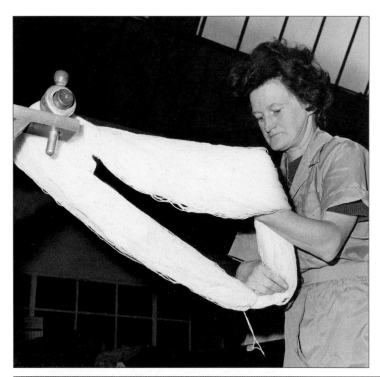

At Patons and Baldwins' Darlington factory the method of training varied from process to process, the basic period being eight weeks. Seen here on 1 March 1962, an operative is handling a skein of wool, getting a feel for the job.

According to Mr John Raybould, personnel manager at Patons' Darlington factory in the 1960s, if the management was such that people took a pride in the job they were doing, then it was good management. At Patons, the people closest to the workers on the factory floor, those who meant most to a new employee, were the trainers and foremen. Pictured here in October 1963, a trainer is explaining the system to an operative.

First impressions are most important – a fact well known to Patons and Baldwins. The entrance hall of the administrative building at their Darlington factory, seen here on 13 January 1965, was designed to put visitors in a happy frame of mind.

Late in 1960 a 'marriage' was arranged between Patons and Baldwins of Darlington and J. and P. Coates of Paisley, two of the leading concerns in the wool and cotton trades. It was the richest merger in the textile industry. The companies were worth £130 million in assets and covered a combined market capital valuation of over £106 million. The two companies had worked in harmony in the export markets and the news of this merger was unexpected in the City, although in August 1959 J. and P. Coates had taken over from Patons and Baldwins a quarter-share interest in Fleming Reid, the 'Scotch Wool Shop' group. The merger brought new importance to 'cotton wool', and, as this view from Patons' factory canteen and social centre shows, everything in the garden was lovely.

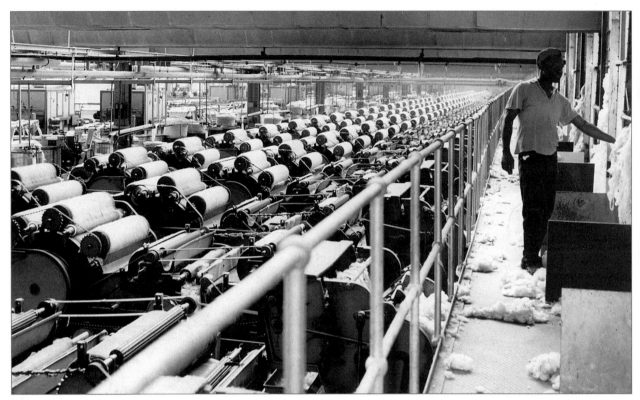

Wool being spun at Patons and Baldwins' Darlington factory under the supervision of a machine minder, 31 August 1966.

A line of Patons and Baldwins' lorries at the Darlington factory on 30 September 1967, bound for destinations throughout the United Kingdom.

Mrs Marjory Johnson of Darlington, pictured here in 1968, came straight to Patons and Baldwins from school. The firm had been in Darlington for only two years when she began working there and everyone was fairly inexperienced. This vivacious lady with her ever-ready smile had a natural aptitude for her job, which she enjoyed. These qualities stood her in good stead and promotion soon came along. When this picture was taken she was the senior training instructor at the factory.

Mr G.W. Rochester, training manager of the North-East Division, talking into the microphone as trainer Mrs Kathy Hamilton keeps a watchful eye on Teresa Painter during a Dictaphone demonstration at Patons and Baldwins' Darlington factory in 1968.

Patons and Baldwins' Darlington factory was noted for the excellent opportunities it offered to young girls in various departments. Here, pictured on 5 July 1968, Christine Hodson of Sedgefield is with Miss Margaret Coyne, supervisor in the twisting department.

This picture was taken on the same day and shows Jean Grace of Staindrop at work under the supervision of Mrs Kathy Hamilton in the cap twisting section.

Mr Frank Ogden, chief rug designer, pictured in April 1974. Frank was one of the key workers brought to Darlington when Patons and Baldwins moved to the town. He is shown here at his drawing board from which, for over forty years, he produced thousands of best-selling designs for Patons and Baldwins.

During his first forty years with Patons and Baldwins Mr C.P.B. Thomson, assistant manager of the wool office at Darlington, was never late for work. In appreciation of this achievement Patons and Baldwins presented him with a clock. He is seen here in October 1974.

It really needs an aerial photograph to show just how large and complex Patons and Baldwins' Darlington factory is. This picture was taken on 30 July 1976.

As well as having a very large factory, the firm's cheques were sometimes monumental, both in size and content. Here, Robin Harrison, salesman of the year, receives a nice bonus on 25 August 1976.

Trouble at mill! On 21 September 1978 the Patons and Baldwins' workforce staged a one-day strike in response to the company's rejection of a shorter working week.

Over 50,000 third-world children have benefited from a unique programme started by Patons and Baldwins. Kind-hearted knitters used up their oddments to make up simple tops that were donated to Oxfam and distributed all over the world. Patons printed the simple pattern at their Darlington factory and distributed them free of charge. The scheme was a tremendous success.

Janet Young (left) and Cornelia Gracey, two brilliant designers who worked for Patons and Baldwins. They lived in Leeds and commuted daily to work in Darlington – what dedication! They are seen here in February 1983.

This is the man who was at the top of the Patons and Baldwins' tree in 1987, Mr Alistair Henderson, managing director of the company and president of the Confederation of British Wool Textiles Ltd. In 2002 the whole of the Patons and Baldwins' site is controlled by Lingfield Warehouses. While Patons and Baldwins no longer produce wool here, the company runs a distribution centre from the site.

6

Rothmans

Louis Rothman was born in the Ukraine in 1869. As a boy he was sent to work in his uncle's
large tobacco factory near Kiev where he acquired his knowledge of tobacco and tobacco
blending which was later to make him one of the world's master blenders. He emigrated to
England in 1887 and at the age of twenty-one, with capital of just £40, founded the Rothmans
business in small premises in Fleet Street. In 1900 he acquired a shop in Pall Mall, which gave its
name to the famous brand of cigarettes introduced at that time to Buckingham Palace, well-
known London clubs and many export markets. On Louis Rothman's death in 1926, the business
was carried on by his son Sydney, who formed the public company in 1929. Only the finest
quality tobacco is used by Carreras Rothmans. When taken from the crates, as seen here in
1977, the compressed tobacco could weigh between 400 and 450 lb a block.

At the beginning of November 1976, Carreras Rothmans confirmed that it would be taking over part of the 500,000 sq. ft of Patons and Baldwins' Darlington site and would be in production before Christmas. The announcement was made from their Basildon factory, pictured here in 1977, with the Famous Black Cat standing guard outside. By February 1977 the Darlington factory was employing about 400 people, and this figure rose to a thousand in the following few months as production built up to 1,000 million cigarettes a month.

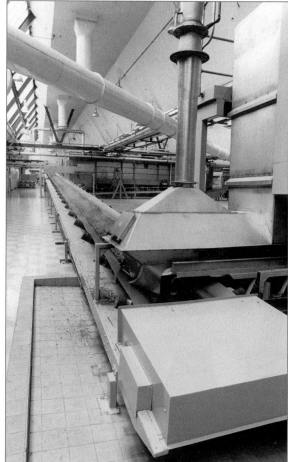

Most of the cigarettes produced at the Darlington factory today are Rothmans King Size and are for export.

Sheikh Ahmed Naghi of Saudi
Arabia, the main distributor of
Rothmans cigarettes in the Middle
East, is pictured here on 3 August
1978 with (left) Mr Graham
Johnson, production manager, and
Mr Cedric Bramston, operations
manager, during the sheikh's visit
to the Darlington factory.

Rothmans' promise of a thousand new jobs for Darlington was greeted with delight by the unemployed and the trade unions but long-established firms viewed the prospect with horror because their pay rates were pegged by law and they feared that Rothmans' higher wages would draw away the area's much-needed skilled workers. Rates of pay offered by the tobacco giant were far above that provided by many local factories. No wonder Rothmans' brass band members, pictured here in 1978, were blowing their trumpets.

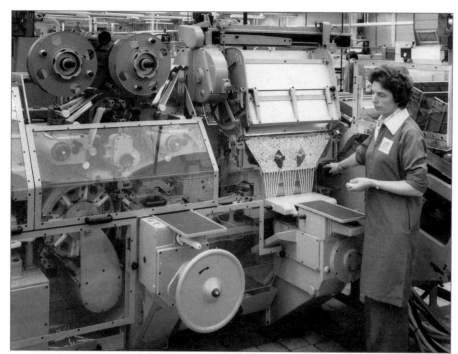

Mrs Mary Mallam at work in the Rothmans factory, December 1978. The machine could turn out 360 packets of 20 cigarettes every minute.

In July 1980 Carreras Rothmans presented a cheque for £250 to the Darlington branch of the Workers Educational Association in support of their work at Bennet House, Darlington. George Flynn (centre right), chairman of the branch, received the cheque from Ian Warrington (centre left), operations manager at Rothmans' Darlington factory.

Councillor Allan Gill, the Mayor of Darlington, taking a close look at the Rothmans' tank engine, 28 May 1978. He is escorted by Mr Ian Warrington, Rothmans operations manager.

James Lester MP on a visit to Rothmans' Darlington factory in July 1980. He is being shown how to roll his own 'ticklers'.

From its early days Rothmans International took its place among the world's leading multi-national tobacco companies. Rothmans of Pall Mall (International), of which the factory at Darlington was a part, was the Group's main export department. The Group's most important assets were its brands and its employees. With about 17,000 employees worldwide, particular attention was given to developing and maintaining an experienced base of international managers who were well trained and highly motivated. Pictured here in August 1980 are some Malaysians from Rothmans' Kuala Lumpur factory on a training course at the Darlington factory with instructor David Kilpatrick.

In collaboration with the *Northern Echo*, Carreras Rothmans staged an art competition in April 1981. Admiring one of the exhibits are, from left to right, Sara Leigh, the Earl of Lichfield, Mr Davies, Mr Warrington and Don Evans.

Carreras Rothmans received a Queen's Award for Export Achievement in April 1983. During the subsequent celebrations Councillor Bill Newton, the Mayor of Darlington, is pictured raising the British Safety Council flag while six men from the RAF Regimental Band sound a fanfare. Appreciative Rothmans employees watch the proceedings.

John Recker (left), the manager of Woolworths in Darlington, receives a special delivery on 4 July 1983 from David Pollard of Rothmans, as part of the special events marking the Rothmans open day.

Taking part in London's Lord Mayor's Show in November 1983 is Lynda Baty of Staindrop, wearing Victorian dress. She is pictured with Pell and Mell, the 8-year-old Irish hunters that pulled the 118-year-old Rothmans of Pall Mall brougham through the City of London. Spoken with an upper crust accent, 'Pell' and 'Mell' together form 'Pall Mall'.

A convivial Japanese delegation samples some Pall Mall cigarettes at Rothmans' Darlington factory, July 1984. Vernon Wilson (left) and Gerry Osborne (right) are not smoking, perhaps because cigarettes made here are for export, not home consumption. Commercial correctness can sometimes be carried too far!

Winner of the Rothmans Graduate and Business Development Awards in 1986 was Susan Bidmead of Durham, seen here on 23 July 1986 with Magnus Magnusson.

Ann Jopling, a packer at Rothmans' Darlington factory, pictured with the 100 millionth packet on 5 June 1986.

The presentation of the 1987 National Training Awards in Newcastle. Left to right: Jim Wilkinson (operations/personnel manager, Rothmans), Paul Neate (director of operations, Rothmans), Mark Weston (regional director, MSC), John Cope (Minister of State for Employment), Derek King (general manager, UK Manufacturing, Rothmans), Colin Neill (training and development manager, Rothmans).

During the open day at Rothmans' Darlington factory on 29 June 1987 firemen demonstrated their rescue skills on some unfortunate Rothmans' workers!

Within the Carreras Rothmans organisation excellence has always been acknowledged and rewarded. Here Colin Wood (left), Michael Keelty (second right) and David Dixon (right) have received their Awards for Excellence from David Grant, Lord Lieutenant of County Durham.

Tobacco being carried along a conveyor in Rothmans' Darlington factory in the late 1980s. Rothmans was one of the Rothmans International Group's three trade marks, the other two being Dunhill and Peter Stuyvesant. All three were among the top fifteen international trade marks in the world.

The last stages of the cigarette production line at Rothmans' Darlington factory in the mid-1980s. Thousands of Rothmans King Size wait to be put into packets – anybody got a match?

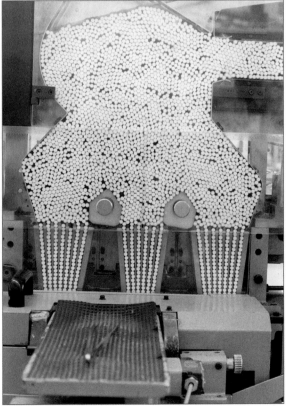

Mr Paul Neate, director of manufacturing at Rothmans' Darlington factory, explaining some of the finer points of tobacco selection to Councillor Ken Fairer, the Mayor of Darlington, on 21 March 1987. It was here that the quality of the cigarette was decided. Assessing tobacco was a highly skilled job.

Councillor David Lyonette, the Mayor of Darlington, being shown the first stage of the cigarette production line by Dessie Johnston, factory manager at Rothmans' Darlington factory, on 9 March 1993.

7

Two Mills & A Forge

Joseph Pease (1788–1872), seen here, was Darlington's most famous son. He was the largest coal owner in the north-east, the first Quaker MP and the financial brain behind the Stockton & Darlington Railway. His son Arthur Pease (1837–98) was a councillor for thirty-one years, Mayor of Darlington and a Unionist MP. His son was Sir Arthur Francis Pease (1866–1927), a director of the NER and chairman of Pease & Partners Ltd. His son, Sir Richard Arthur Pease (1890–1957), was a director of Pease & Partners, chairman of the governors of Darlington Training College and the first chairman of Tyne Tees Television. His eldest son, Arthur Peter Pease (1918–40), flew Spitfires with 603 Squadron during the Second World War and was killed in action. Sir Richard's second son, Sir Richard Thorn Pease, was born in 1922 and went on to become chairman of Yorkshire Bank. The Pease family is one of great renown and has served Darlington in an exemplary manner. No industrial history of Darlington would be complete without mention of this family.

The first Edward Pease, born in 1711, worked in Darlington for his uncle Thomas Cauldwell, a wool comber, taking over and expanding the business to encompass dyeing and weaving when his uncle died. When Edward Pease died in 1785 his son Joseph took control of two mills on the River Skerne, one in the Leadyard and a larger one in Priestgate, seen in its heyday in the photograph above. In the early part of the nineteenth century at least 10 per cent of Darlington's population was employed in the wool mills of what had become H. Pease & Company. In those early days the mill was more a centre for exchange than for manufacture. Wool was bought in the country districts and brought to the mill for sorting, washing and cleaning. It was then handed out to the wool combers who combed it in their own cottages. When the work was done they returned the wool to the mill and were paid on commission. A similar procedure was adopted for spinning. The combed wool was distributed to workers' cottages, from where the noise of numerous spinning machines could be heard. Gradually machinery was acquired, buildings erected and the industry that was to mean so much to Darlington grew into a live and prosperous undertaking, becoming one of the chief supports of the town. The mill chimney seen on the right was built between 1874 and 1875. It had the distinction of having been built by donkey power! A pulley and rope attached to the donkey was used to lift bricks up to the men working on the chimney, which was built from the inside and reached a height of 130 ft.

Towards the end of the eighteenth century the two brothers Edward and Joseph succeeded to the business, which in 1817 received a severe blow through the destruction of the Leadyard Mill by fire, which caused £30,000-worth of damage and put 600 people out of work. At that time the population of Darlington was 6,551. The firm, now called Joseph Pease & Sons, gradually recovered from the fire and quickly gained a reputation for fine craftsmanship. Many awards were gained by Pease's Mills at exhibitions in London, Bradford, New York and Brussels. The firm also won awards at the 1851 Great Exhibition held at Crystal Palace and later had the honour of manufacturing dress material for Queen Alexandra. In 1837 the Peases built their Railway Mill in Northgate. It included the first weaving sheds in Darlington, containing 400 looms which continued in production until 1891. The weaving shed time bell was rung until 1918 when its last peals told of the arrival of peace. On 26 February 1894 Pease's Priestgate Mill was ravaged by fire, which caused £20,000-worth of damage. Pictured above is the mill after the fire, showing the old stone bridge over the River Skerne and the piles for the building of the present one.

Strong sunshine cannot dispel the gloom surrounding this dejected group, come to see the damage at Priestgate Mill following the 1894 fire.

Margaret Grey, ninety-one years old when this picture
was taken in 1982, used to work at Pease's Mill. The old
custom of tolling the mill bell 5 minutes before work was
due to start in the morning and the afternoon
summoned her and the other workers to their tasks. In
the early days of the mill, most of the workers lived
within 5 minutes of the mill and could hear the bell from
their home.

From 1752 to 1902 the business was owned by a series
of partnerships, all involving the Pease family. In 1903
the firm became a private limited company with some of
the Pease family on the board of directors. For many
years a very happy business relationship had existed
between Henry Pease & Co. Ltd and Lister & Co. Ltd of
Bradford. In 1920 Lister purchased all the share capital
of Henry Pease & Co. Ltd and appointed a new board of
directors. To all outward appearances the mills seemed
the same as they had been fifty years before but inside,
considerable improvements had been made. Electricity
had supplanted steam power and the machines were
now driven by individual motors. New machinery had
replaced the old. Sadly, on Sunday 2 July 1933, the
wool warehouse at Pease's Mill burst into flames. The
fire raged for 8 hours. Water from the River Skerne was
used to supplement the town water from the hydrants;
the firemen's efforts managed to save the machinery, but
all the raw material was destroyed and only the shell of
the building remained. Thanks to the availability of
modern transport, and the goodwill of their friends in
Bradford, raw material was available the next day and
there was no loss of employment.

Pease's Priestgate Mill viewed from the mill's small garden, *c. 1930*. At the beginning of the Second World War Pease's Mills played an indirect part in the sinking of the German raider *Graf Spee*. A consignment of wool for Pease's Darlington mill was shipped out of Australia on the *Doric Star*, whose cargo consisted mainly of victuals. The German raider *Graf Spee*, itself low on supplies, stopped the *Doric Star*, whose crew used the wool to conceal the victuals she was carrying. It was a successful ruse and the German boarding party never found the victuals. Having abandoned the *Doric Star*, the Germans sank it, but this situation brought the *Graf Spee* within range of the British warships that destroyed it. In the first few days of the Second World War the workers at Pease's Mills, with the help of a few volunteers, assembled 60,000 gas masks for the civilian population in less than 60 hours.

Opposite: On 14 July 1964 Mr Harry Smith, general manager of Henry Pease & Co. Ltd, announced that 'Pease's Mill, Darlington, will run their machinery to the last minute before leaving their doomed building in Priestgate'. He added that 'the combing machinery will, in due course, be transferred to another group mill in Bradford where better facilities exist for wool combing'. On 23 September 1964 demolition contractors were busy pulling down a section of Pease's Mill in Priestgate, Darlington, as pictured here.

DARLINGTON & SIMPSON ROLLING MILLS LTD

Darlington & Simpson Rolling Mills Ltd was originally called Fry I'Anson & Co. Its Rise Carr Works were built in 1862–3, opened in 1864 and 'the roof blew off in 1865'. The original works consisted of a puddling forge, which converted pig iron to wrought iron by heating it with ferric oxide in a furnace to oxidise the carbon, one 16-ft mill and one 10-ft mill. Iron was the only product. In about 1870 an 8-ft mill and another puddling forge were added. By the turn of the twentieth century steel had begun to supersede iron and the works began to roll steel sections instead, as seen here.

Window frames packed up ready for dispatch to Africa, in 1975.

Darlington & Simpson Rolling Mills Ltd occupied three sites which were designated the South, North and West Works. In 1902 a rivet manufacturing shop was erected at the extreme north end of the South Works. In 1930 it was removed to the North Works to make room for Nos 1 and 2 yards. In 1904 a mill was laid down for the rolling of light rails from old rails and billet crops. A forge was dismantled to make room for this mill. Here we see rails being rolled in 1968.

Overleaf: In 1904 Fry I'Anson & Co.'s name was changed to Sir Theodore Fry & Co. and in 1910 the name changed again to Darlington Rolling Mills Co. Ltd. Of the company's three sites, South Works, pictured here in 1974, occupied 5.47 acres and was the smallest; North Works occupied 9.4 acres and West Works, the largest, occupied 15.74 acres. In 1911 there was a complete regrouping of Rise Carr Works. Everything was electrified except the 8-ft mill, which continued to run under steam until it was dismantled in about 1924. In 1917 a new Rail Mill was built to the north of the existing works. Then came the 1920s, which were dark days for Darlington Rolling Mills, because of competition from cheaper continental steel imports. A full week's work had become a thing of the past.

In 1933 Mr George Whitehouse joined the firm as a roll-shop worker. On 23 June 1980 he was presented with a wallet and notes by manager Mr George Watson on his retirement after forty-seven years.

In 1935 the company once more changed its name, this time to the Darlington & Simpson Rolling Mills Ltd. At that time anyone with ideas about the company kept it to themselves. But times change: here Dr David Pugh (left), general manager, manufacturing, is presenting a cheque to Mr Jim Barnes, winner of the company's suggestion award, on 16 June 1985.

During an industrial dispute in 1980, strikers are busy ordering more pints. Some want five! It's thirsty work, striking.

In January 1982 it was business as usual inside Darlington & Simpson Rolling Mills.

Outside the Rolling Mills, everything in the garden was lovely. Here we see Mr John Carter, the firm's managing director, with Graeme Alderson of the BBC's *Townscape* programme, on 29 June 1988.

In January 1986 seven members of staff received their twenty-five years service awards from John Carter, the managing director, in the DSRM Sports and Social club. Left to right: Mick Armitt, Jim Freeman, Elizabeth Ireland, Jack Simpson, John Carter, Barry Griffiths, Dick Marshall and Jim Barnes. Another man, Ernie Hopper, also received an award but was unable to attend the ceremony. In 1998 Darlington & Simpson Rolling Mills Ltd closed down.

THE DARLINGTON FORGE LTD

From small beginnings in about 1850 the Darlington Forge Ltd built up a worldwide reputation in the application of scientific heat treatment to large steel forgings and castings, necessitating more accurately controlled temperatures. Pictured here in 1939 are some of the Forge personnel who, in their varied jobs, made the company tick. All these men are members of the Forge's ambulance team.

A boiler drum being produced at Darlington Forge Ltd, 1965. Such items were for land and marine boilers. In addition hollow-forged, high-pressure vessels for oil and chemical processes were also manufactured by the company.

Darlington Forge Ltd, *c.* 1950. The company produced major parts for some of the finest ships built in the first half of the twentieth century and enjoyed close associations with such well-known ships as the *Mauretania*, the *Lusitania*, the *Aquitania*, the *Majestic*, HMS *Nelson* and the *Queen Mary*.

In 1936 the British passenger liner *Queen Mary* was built for the Cunard shipping line. Darlington Forge Ltd constructed the liner's stern frame, pictured here. It was the largest cast-steel stern frame ever made and weighed 190 tons.

Early in 1965 the MV *Tripolis* broke down in the Mediterranean and had to be towed to Skaramanga in Greece. During the tow, the rudder suffered serious damage. Messages went round the world for a fast delivery of a new rudder stock and, against fierce competition, the Forge won the order by offering a better delivery date. Astonishingly, they even smashed their own promises, and the rudder stock, pictured here, left the Forge five days ahead of the nine-week delivery schedule.

A boiler drum being manufactured. The small main bearings for Sydney Harbour Bridge in New South Wales, Australia, were built at Darlington Forge for re-erection on site at Sydney. Their finished weight was 300 tons each. The firm also built corresponding bearings for the Tyne Bridge, weighing 32 tons each.

The old machine shop at the Darlington Forge Ltd, pictured here in 1972, is empty of machines but is filled with fond memories of proud achievements and good comradeship. When a factory like the Darlington Forge is demolished, generations of people associated with it also fade away, consigned to history and soon forgotten by future generations. This is sad because it is through the achievements of our forebears that our lives are enriched.

8

The Northern Echo

On 1 January 1870 the first edition of the *Northern Echo*, founded by John Hyslop Bell, went on sale. It was a campaigning Liberal morning newspaper, published 'to supply a want of the age and district, viz, a well conducted, high class, daily newspaper advocating advanced Liberal opinions and published at a price which will bring it within reach of all classes of people'. It was sold for just ½*d*. While abroad, John Hyslop Bell read an article about Christianity in a democracy which so impressed him that, on his return to England, he determined to find out more about the author, W.T. Stead, who is pictured here. He turned out to be a young man from Embleton, near Alnwick, then working as a journalist in Newcastle. Hyslop Bell met him and W.T. Stead was offered the job of editor of the *Northern Echo*, which he accepted. It was a noteworthy decision. W.T. Stead was an outstanding editor, 'with printer's ink in his veins'. He was editor of the *Northern Echo* from 1871 until 1880. He lost his life while a passenger on the White Star Liner *Titanic* when it hit an iceberg and sank on 14 April 1912.

The *Northern Echo*'s first home was a rented office in a former thread and shoe lace factory. From there W.T. Stead set about 'attacking the devil' in his various guises, laxity of morals and prostitution being two of them. His strong views brought him into conflict with the Quakers, whose money had originally established the *Northern Echo*. However, one might say it was the right paper at the right time; in fact, everything was right – the price was right, the right man was at the helm and it had the Wright outlets!

The Northern Echo

Founded 1869—First Halfpenny Morning Paper in the World.

NEWCASTLE, TUESDAY, 19 APRIL, 1904.

DANISH VISIT ENDS.	MULLAH CHASE	AT LAST!	LIBEL SUIT.	THE BISHOPS' PROTE

This copy of the *Northern Echo* erroneously states that the newspaper was founded in 1869 when the actual date was 1 January 1870. The confusion arose because it was in about June 1869 that John Hyslop Bell set about establishing this great newspaper. This mistake was finally corrected on 26 April 1967, from which date the headline 'Founded 1870' was used.

In 1908 the *Northern Echo* bought its rented offices. In 1914 the *Darlington Evening Despatch* was founded to keep the public up to date with the war news. In 1915 the present *Northern Echo* building was under construction, as seen here. In 1928 the *Darlington Evening Despatch* changed its name to the *Northern Despatch*. Then three papers from the same stable, the *Northern Echo*, the *Darlington and Stockton Times* and the *Northern Despatch*, were merged into the Starmer group of newspapers. Sir Charles Starmer was twice Mayor of Darlington.

It was from its new home, on 12 November 1918, that the *Northern Echo* announced the joyous news that Germany had surrendered and the war was over.

In 1932 the *Northern Echo* created a most charming and popular children's feature. The Nignogs sprinkled stardust and magic on to childhood, and even helped establish the Nignog Ward to support those children afflicted by illness.

In 1945 Reginald Gray became the only Darlingtonian to occupy the editorial chair of the *Northern Echo*, a position he held until 1960. He regarded the *Northern Echo* as a 'weekly published daily', covering world affairs and local news. It was a good mix that did the paper no harm with the local readership. When Reggie Gray retired on 1 January 1961, Shannan Stevenson, managing director of the North of England Newspaper Company Ltd, which now owned the *Echo*, praised him for 'his absolute and determined conviction that the prosperity of the paper lay in its policy of continuing to give a new service of local and regional news'. Under Mark Barrington-Ward, who succeeded Reginald Gray and held the editorial position for eighteen months, the *Northern Echo* failed to move with the times. Then along came Harold Evans, pictured here, and he put the *Northern Echo* on the map.

Following the death of Sir Charles Starmer in 1933, Westminster Press moved its base to Fleet Street and the *Northern Echo*'s editorial power deteriorated. During the Second World War the paper did not even have an emergency plan if its Priestgate presses and offices were bombed. Yet it retained a nucleus of loyal readers, like Jack McMahon, pictured here in 1983, who read the *Northern Echo* every day for over fifty years. Circulation figures rose steadily from just over 83,000 copies a year in 1939 to more than 120,000 in 1952.

Harold Evans joined the *Northern Echo* in 1961, fresh from teaching journalism in India. He brought with him an unusual gift for recognising good writing and good sub-editing. He found the *Northern Echo* 'absolutely solid in its attitude to the region but lacking a vigorous editorial page. A rocket needs a solid base,' he said, 'and the *Northern Echo* was deeply rooted in the region. All I had to do was put some fuel in the engine and nobody had done that for a long time.' Within five-and-a-half heady years Harold Evans had so improved the *Northern Echo* that it was talked about in the corridors of power in a way not seen since the days of W.T. Stead. So it is that whenever a stranger to the region asks about the fine building on the corner of Priestgate and Crown Street in Darlington, the usual reply, spoken with pride, is 'That's the home of the *Northern Echo* – top for regional and local news!'

News, hard facts and well-informed comment presented with speed, clarity and simplicity are the lifeblood of any newspaper. Pictured here, using the latest technology, are some of the *Northern Echo*'s news team. But the *Northern Echo* has always enjoyed a wider involvement with local affairs. In 1987, for example, Durham City's City In Bloom competition was entirely sponsored by the *Northern Echo*, which provided the trophies for the ten categories. Each winner also received a City Plaque, suitably inscribed, for them to keep. The *Northern Echo* also provided £350 sponsorship money for prizes, including £100 for the school category. Every year the *Northern Echo*'s office building is festooned with flowers, adding colour and cheer to Darlington.

The *Northern Echo* is no slouch when it comes to giving practical help to the deserving needy whether at home or abroad. In May 1990 it was much involved in organising a convoy of humanitarian supplies being sent from Newcastle to Romania. Seen here are Peter Sands, editor of the *Northern Echo*, and Yvonne Ridley, assistant news editor, with a special Romanian edition of the *Northern Echo* that was sent to Romania with the other supplies. It carries a greetings headline from the *Echo* and its readers.

Dehydration is the journalist's curse and the *Northern Echo*'s award-winning columnist Mike Amos (centre) will go to great lengths to avoid it. On this occasion he went to the opening of the first Weardale Beer Festival. He is pictured here with the organisers Graham Ross (left) and Peter Nattrass, trying the first drinks. It's all in the line of duty, you understand.

In 1990 Peter Sands (third from left), editor of the *Northern Echo*, proudly accepts on behalf of the *Northern Echo* an award acknowledging his paper's involvement in sports work with the handicapped. He is standing between Linford Christie and Nick Helliwell, with Duncan Goodhew second from the right. The names of the lady on the far left and the gentleman on the far right are not known.

Awards for involvement in community matters are very acceptable, but for a newspaper the most prestigious award is one that comes from the newspaper industry itself. This 1992 Newspaper Industry award was given to the *Northern Echo* for newspaper design.

Today, Peter Barron is the deserving occupier of W.T. Stead's famous chair and, like its original owner, he has printer's ink in his veins, though he would be the last to admit it. A strong editor, not afraid to crusade vigorously against injustice, he is deeply concerned for people and the environment and, perhaps best of all, he fervently believes that the strength of a community depends on the strength of its family life. W.T. Stead and Peter Barron have much in common. In this picture this successful editor of the *Northern Echo* appears in a relaxed mood with his beautiful wife and their delightful children. The future of his family and of the *Northern Echo* are in safe hands. Unlike so many of Darlington's industries, the newspaper industry has weathered the storms of time and, with Peter Barron at the helm, the newspaper of the north faces the future with confidence.